Carving
Golf Ball Spirits

Tom Wolfe

Text written with and photography
by Jeffrey B. Snyder

Schiffer Publishing Ltd

4880 Lower Valley Road, Atglen, Pa 19310

Other Schiffer Books by Tom Wolfe.
Carving Traditional Woodspirits with Tom Wolfe. ISBN: 088740538X. $12.95.
The Golfers. ISBN: 0887402933. $12.95.
Out to the Ball Game with Tom Wolfe. ISBN: 0887404979. $12.95.
Power Carving House Spirits with Tom Wolfe. ISBN: 0764301837. $12.95.
Tom Wolfe Carves Wood Spirits and Walking Sticks. ISBN: 0887404413. $12.95

Other Schiffer Books on Related Subjects
Carving Fishermen and the Tall Tale. Cleve Taylor. ISBN: 0887409032. $12.95.

Schiffer Books are available at special discounts for bulk purchases for sales promotions or premiums. Special editions, including personalized covers, corporate imprints, and excerpts can be created in large quantities for special needs. For more information contact the publisher:

Published by Schiffer Publishing Ltd.
4880 Lower Valley Road
Atglen, PA 19310
Phone: (610) 593-1777; Fax: (610) 593-2002
E-mail: Info@schifferbooks.com

For the largest selection of fine reference books on this and related subjects, please visit our web site at **www.schifferbooks.com**
We are always looking for people to write books on new and related subjects. If you have an idea for a book please contact us at the above address.

This book may be purchased from the publisher.
Include $5.00 for shipping.
Please try your bookstore first.
You may write for a free catalog.

In Europe, Schiffer books are distributed by
Bushwood Books
6 Marksbury Ave.
Kew Gardens
Surrey TW9 4JF England
Phone: 44 (0) 20 8392-8585; Fax: 44 (0) 20 8392-9876
E-mail: info@bushwoodbooks.co.uk
Website: www.bushwoodbooks.co.uk

Designed by RoS
Type set in Korinna BT/Humanist 521 BT

ISBN: 978-0-7643-3148-0
Printed in China

Contents

Introduction

Have you ever wondered why golf balls act the way they do? There you are, standing right in the middle of a wide, green fairway following a promising tee shot, with an unobstructed, straight line, easy shot you've made a thousand times before lying between you and the green. The day is beautiful. There is no wind. Your spirits soar as you feel your body smoothly answering the call to provide a perfect swing. You connect with the ball … and all hell breaks loose. Veering wildly, that damned ball hooks or slices left or right, careens off three trees, two squirrels, your golf partner and/or a lawyer, and then buries itself deep in the sand trap on the far side of the green. You swear you can hear that miserable little ball chuckling evilly to itself as you approach.

Tom Wolfe knows why. He has discovered all of the evil spirits that reside in the dark hearts of those seemingly innocent and ordinary golf balls. Tom even knows them by name. These wretched creatures are Splash, Splush, Sandy, Woody, The Hooker, Slash, Divot, Swish, Almost, Duckey Hook, Shank, and O'Shit. Each and every one of them lives up to their names.

Follow Tom through the carving and staining steps to come and you too will be able to carve these foul demons in their lairs. Using basic carving tools and a little stain, you'll be able to portray these little beasties, and reveal the truth every golfer has long suspected, to appreciative family, friends, and fellow sufferers on the links.

Carving the Spirits

I'm using a coping saw to cut the surface of the ball all the way around. Of course, I suggest you do this with the ball in a vice.

Stick a small screwdriver into the gap you've created and gently twist the screwdriver to begin lifting the outer coating away from the inner shell.

Like so. Save the top of the shell to work with later.

Sometimes they make nice caps … among other things.

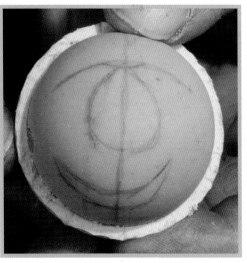

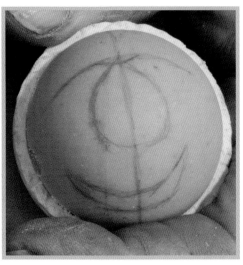

Draw in a centerline and the eye line. Now, the way you draw the eye line will affect the character. An eye line arching upwards leads to a smiling face, while an eye line arching down leads to a frown. Remember, demons laugh a lot.

We're going to give this one a toothy grin. This is almost like carving a pumpkin. V tools and gouges work best for carving golf balls.

I'm using a #9 half round gouge to start.

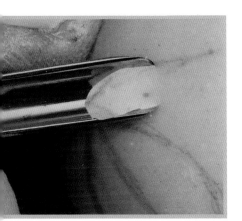

Gouging out an eye socket.

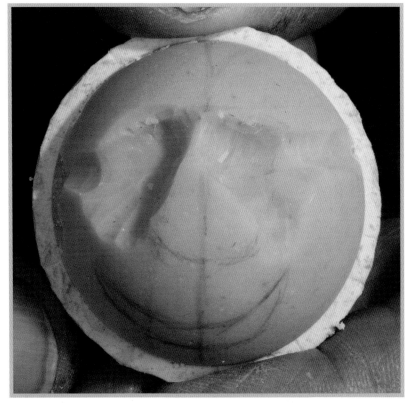

Progress so far. The eye sockets, the outer edges of the nose, and the temples are relieved.

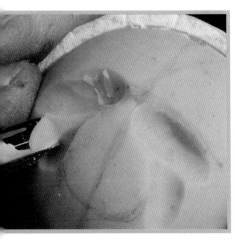

Relieving around the nose. These golf ball spirits are fun to carve. They are quick and easy, almost like "wood carver doodling."

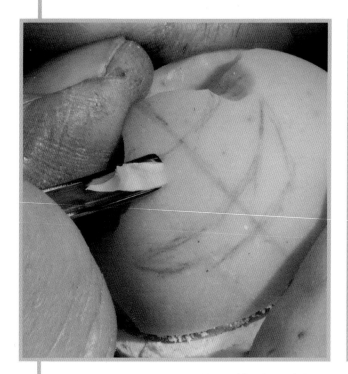 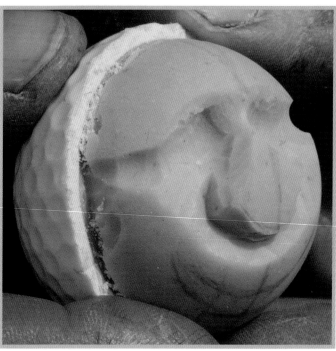

Using a V tool, carefully work beneath the nose to relieve it.

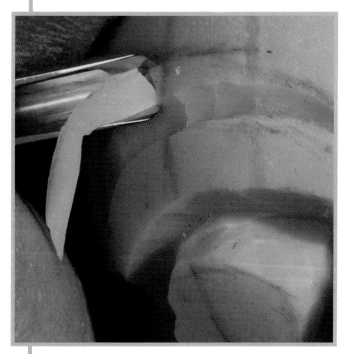

Using the V tool to work around the mouth, looking to create some teeth.

Making an angled cut with the V tool to begin relieving the area of the mouth. The area left in higher relief in the mouth will become the teeth.

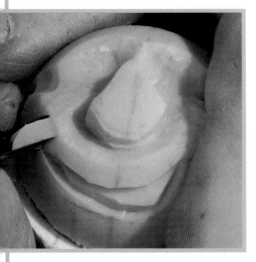

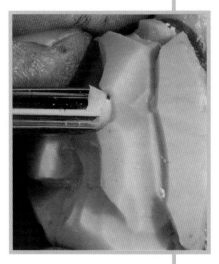

Carving in the smile line, or is it a sneer line? Using the V gouge to create the smile lines.

The smile lines are in place.

Let's add some hair. The hairline is in place. Separate the eyebrows as well.

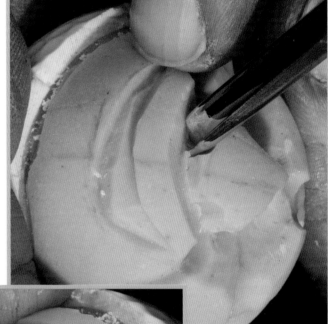

Now we'll take up a knife to put in the detail work. First, use a half round gouge to put in the nostrils and the arioles (the top part of the nostril).

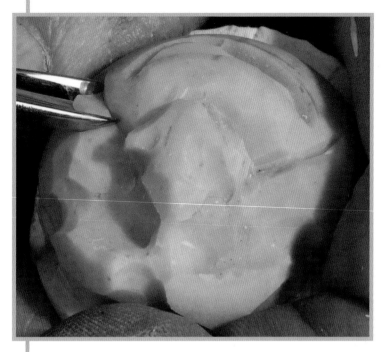 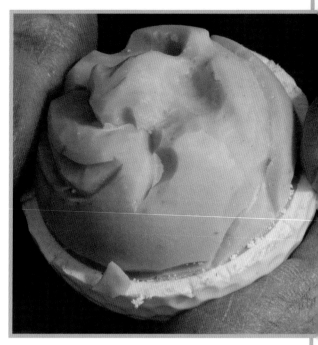

Use the gouge to come in along the outside edge of the smile line to create the cheekbones.

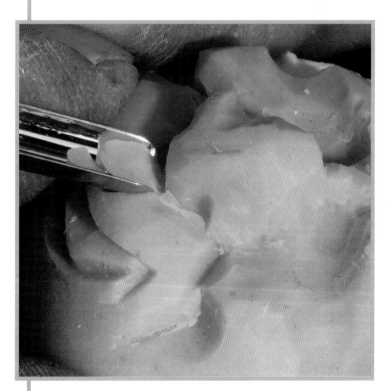 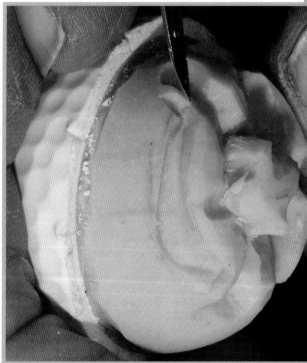

Cutting in the filtrim with a small gouge.

Now we're creating the bow of the upper lips with the knife. First cut a curved line above the lip and then undercut it from the edge of the mouth to finish the lip.

Using the U gouge to create the lower lip. Come in under the upper lip's outer edge to start the cut.

Using the gouge, I'm creating a small chin for the demon, reducing excess stock away around the chin.

Progress.

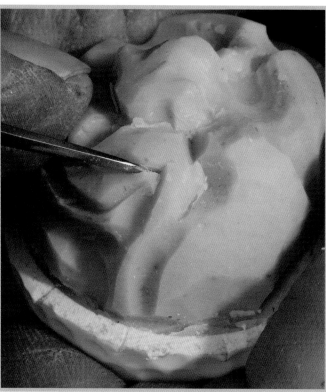

Using a knife, make three cuts into the outer corner of the mouth, cutting out a small triangle in the corner of the mouth to deepen the shadows in the corners of the mouth. One cut goes in on either side of the mouth; the third cut is at the bottom edge of the mouth, cutting in at an angle toward the tip of the mouth to pop out the extra stock. This gives you the deep recess for shadows. Repeat in the other corner of the mouth.

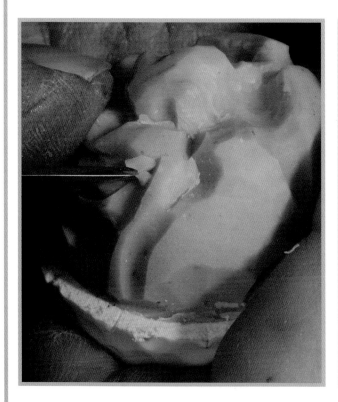
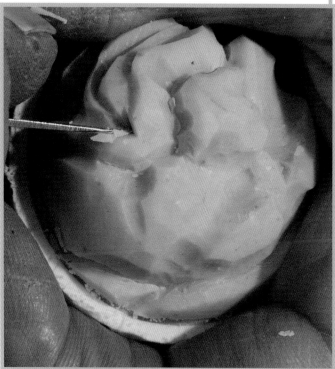

Progress.

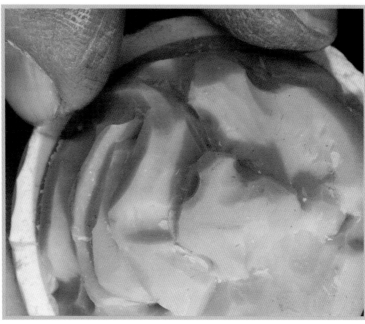

Using a small U gouge to remove a little extra material from above the upper lip to accentuate that upper lip.

Using a small V tool to cut in the teeth.

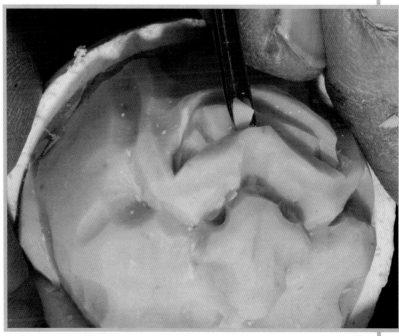

The teeth are in place.

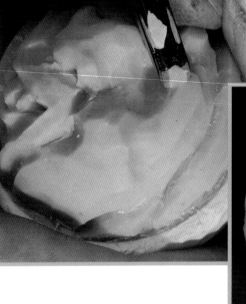

Now we're going to give our demon heavy bags over his eyes. Just a simple arch over the eye in the eyebrow mound creates this effect.

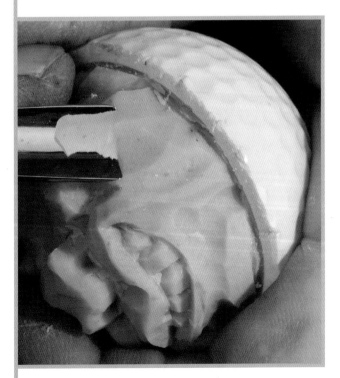

Use a #7 gouge to take out extra fat along the side of the face, along the jaw line.

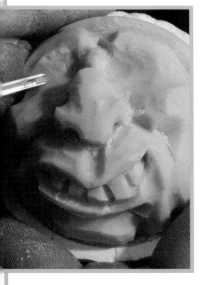

It is time to work on the eyes with a very small V gouge. You can't use a hole punch on these. The first curving cut creates the upper edge of the eye.

Carving in the upper eyelid in an arch above the edge of the eye.

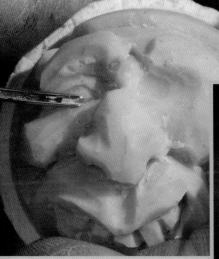

Carving in the lower lid.

Both eyes are in place.

Time to carve the lower lids. Repeat the process for the upper lids.

Like so.

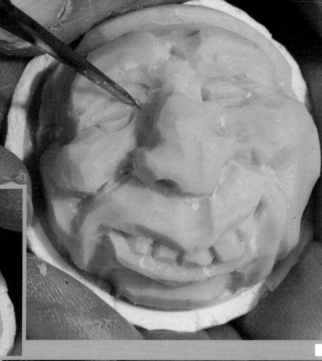

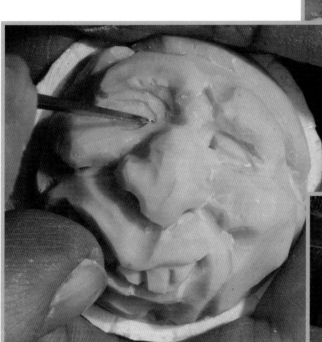

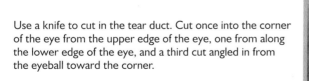

Use a knife to cut in the tear duct. Cut once into the corner of the eye from the upper edge of the eye, one from along the lower edge of the eye, and a third cut angled in from the eyeball toward the corner.

Repeat this process along the outer edge of the eye. Complete both eyes like this.

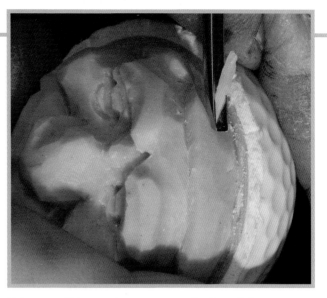

Using a small V gouge, begin carving in the demon's hair.

The hair is carved in.

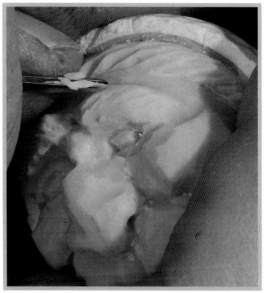

Use a smaller V tool to carve in the hair of the eyebrows.

The hair is in place.

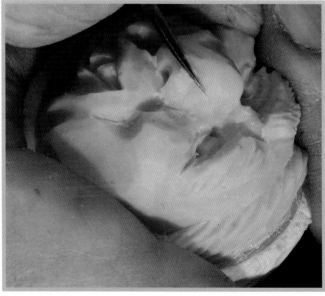

Round down the high points with a knife all around the face.

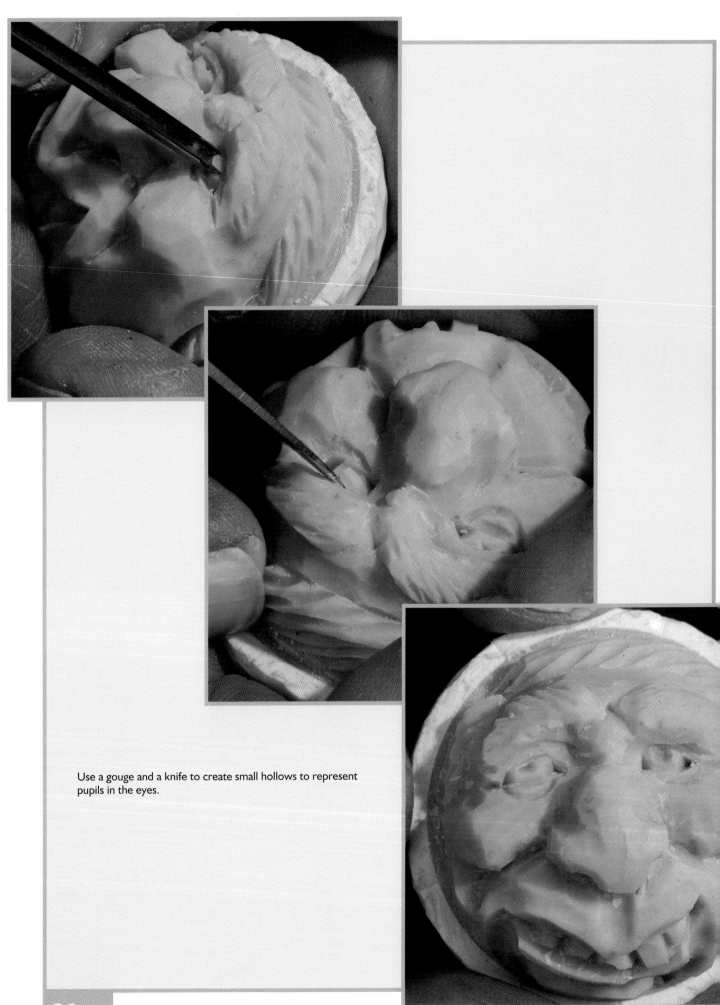

Use a gouge and a knife to create small hollows to represent pupils in the eyes.

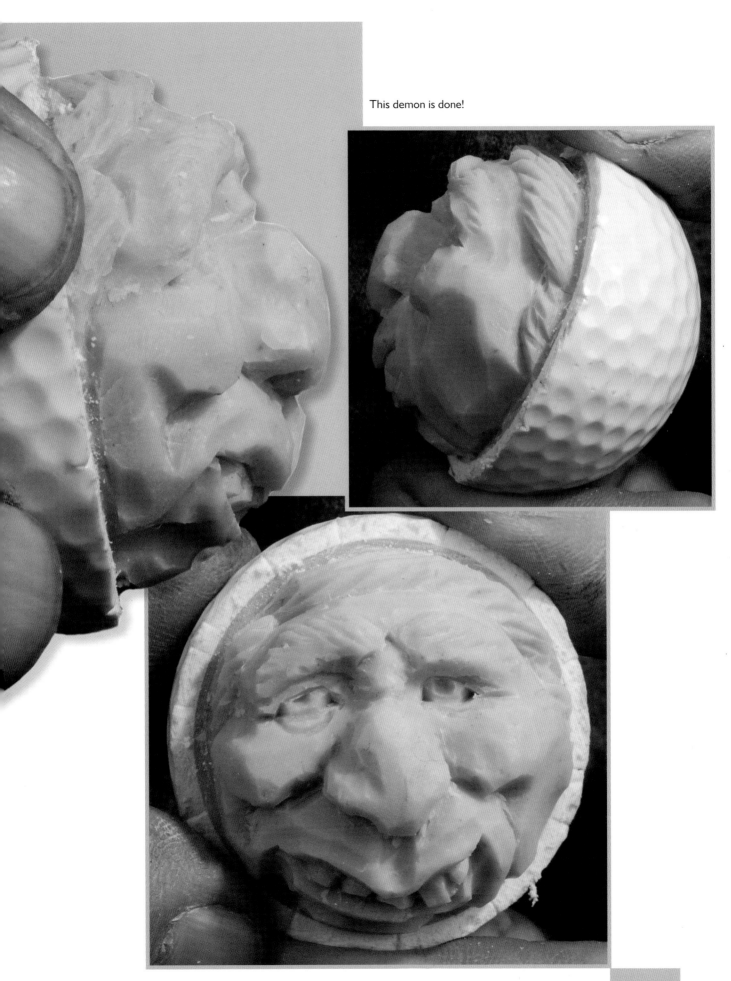

This demon is done!

Let's try it again. Removing half of the outer shell just as before.

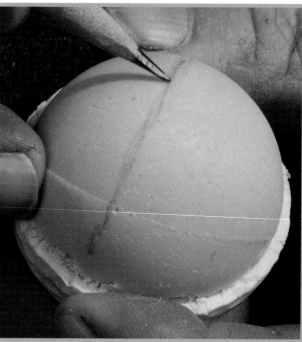

Drawing in the centerline.

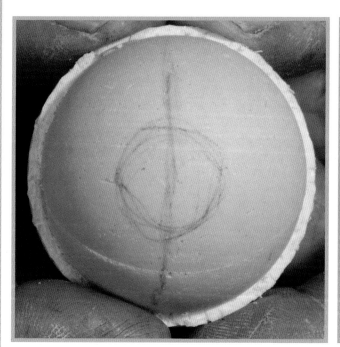

Drawing in a round nose. We'll carve a button nose.

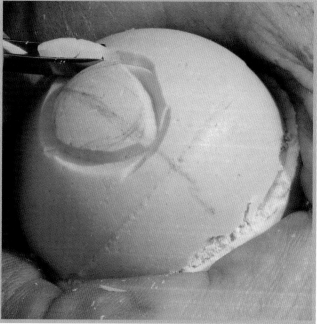

Use a V tool to outline the circle of the nose.

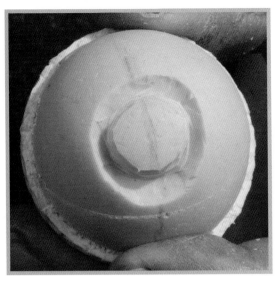

The nose is outlined.

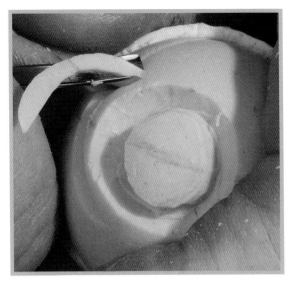

Using the V gouge to begin carving a smiling mouth.

This golf ball demon will have his tongue sticking out the side of his mouth.

Use a half round gouge to hollow out the eye sockets.

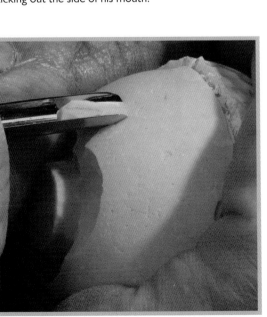

Separating the eyes.

Progress so far.

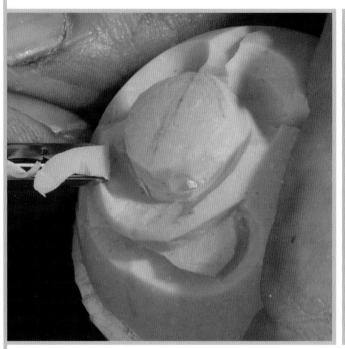

Cutting in the smile lines and beginning to define the temples a bit.

Using a gouge to carve in the lower lip.

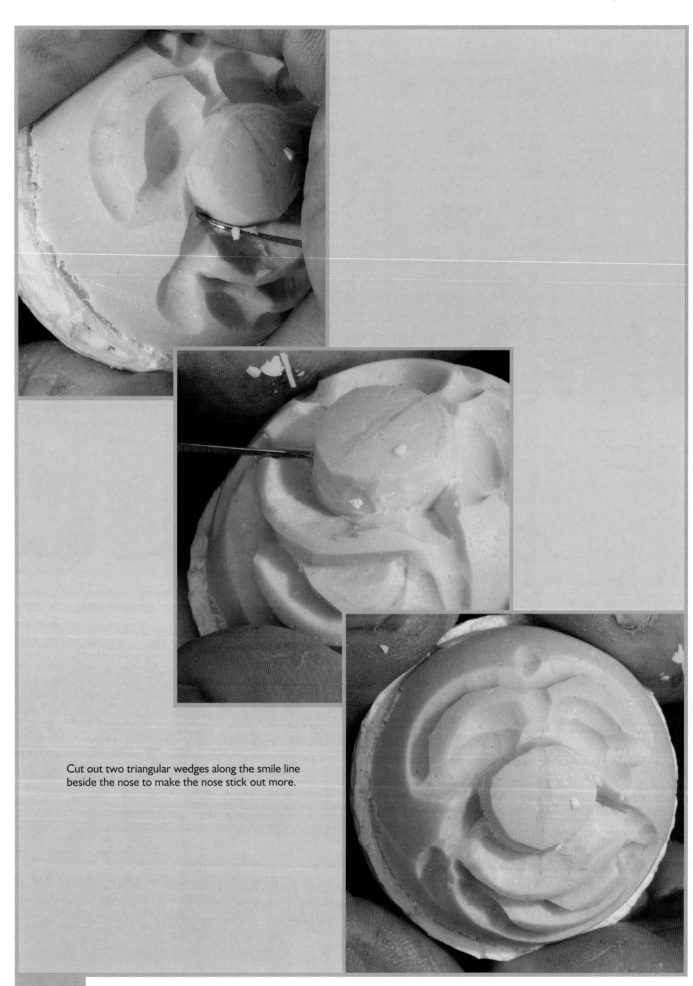

Cut out two triangular wedges along the smile line
beside the nose to make the nose stick out more.

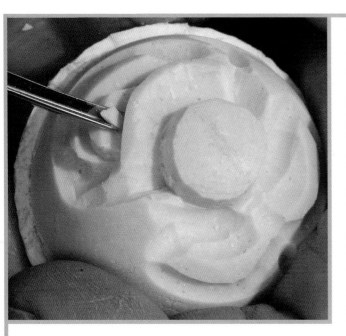

Cutting in the central groove of the tongue.

Like so.

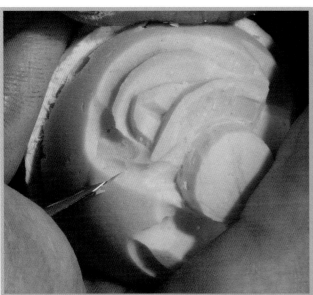

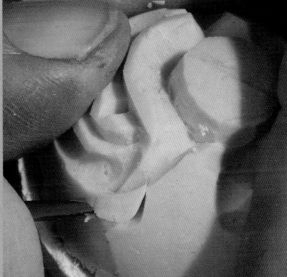

Using the knife, cut along the outside of the smile lines in a curve, cutting back toward the smile line and then pop out the excess material. This will create the cheekbone.

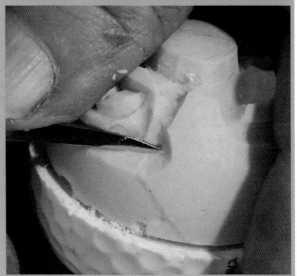

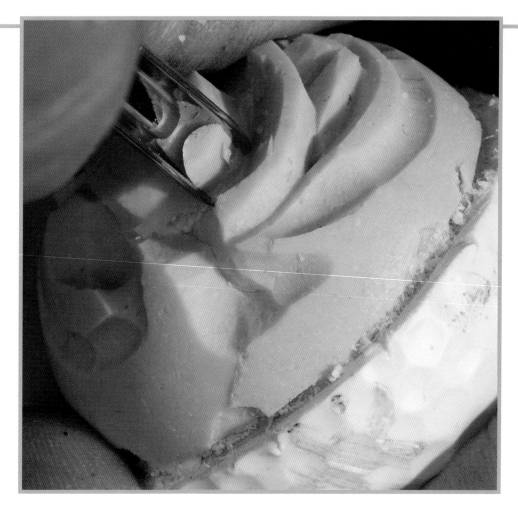

Use a gouge and a knife to cut
out the nostrils.

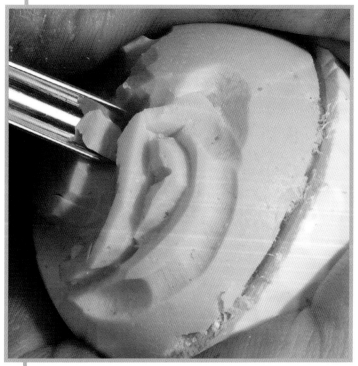

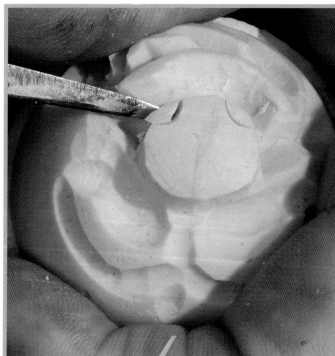

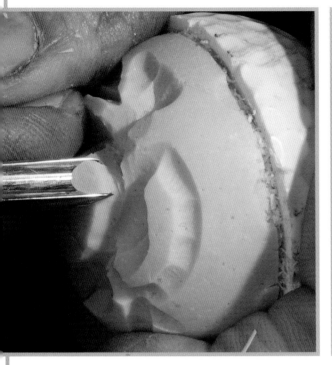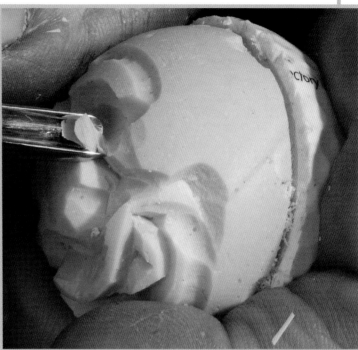

Cut in the arioles, the tops of the nostrils.

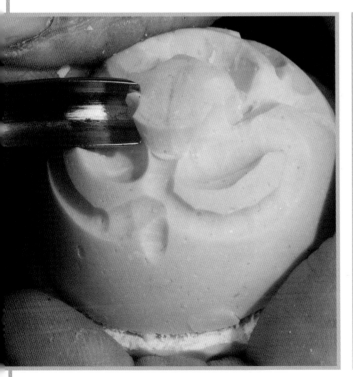

Use a spoon gouge to round down the edges of the nose.

Rounding the nose.

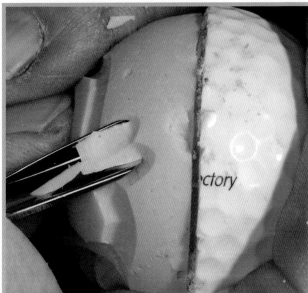

Removing extra material from the area of the temple.

Use a knife to round down the area from the temples on down.

Don't forget to give him a chin. Remove excess
stock from around the small chin.

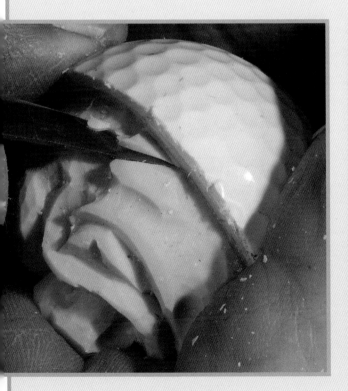

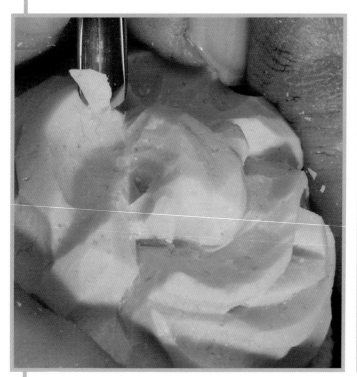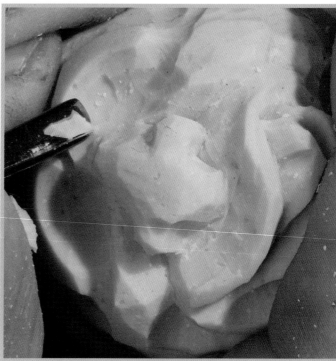

Separate the eyebrows with your gouge.

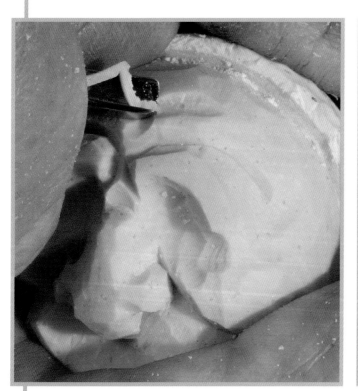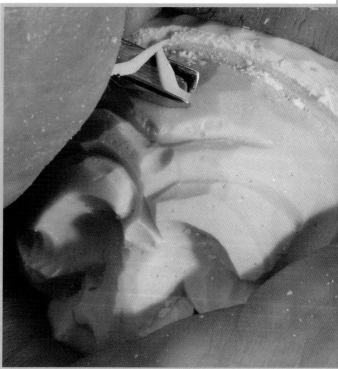

Putting in a couple of wrinkles on his forehead.

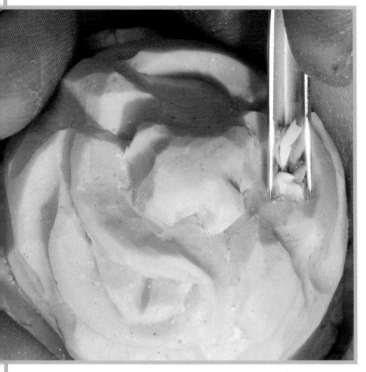 

Deepening the eye sockets to create more shadow.

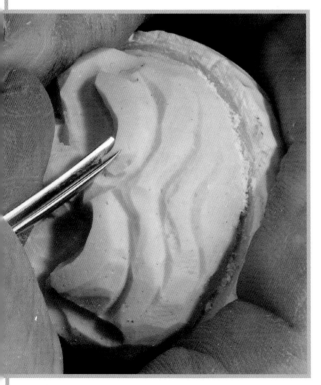 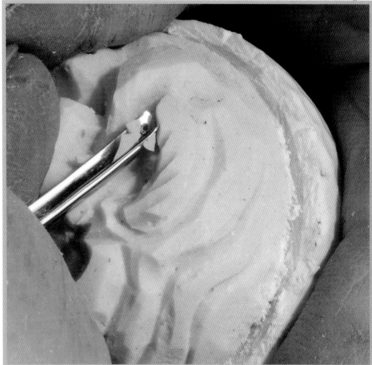

Now it's time to carve in the eyebrows with a V gouge.

The eyebrows are done.

This demon is squinting. Carve in a curved line with the V gouge.

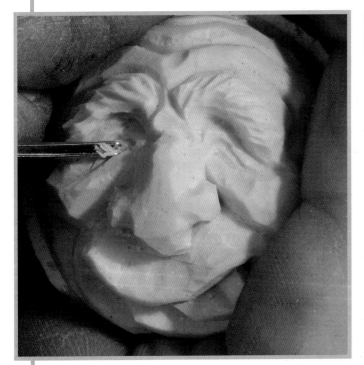

Carve in another line under the eye for the lower lid with the V gouge.

Now to make a stand for the golf ball demon. Drill through the half of the golf ball that was removed earlier.

Use a piece of wood as a based to hold the golf ball half. Drill through the wood so that a golf tee can be run through the golf ball shell and the wooden base.

Staining the Spirits

Now it's time to paint a golf ball demon. Using burnt sienna oil paint thinned with turpentine.

The painted golf ball demon.

Once the paint is applied, spray it with Krylon matte finish.

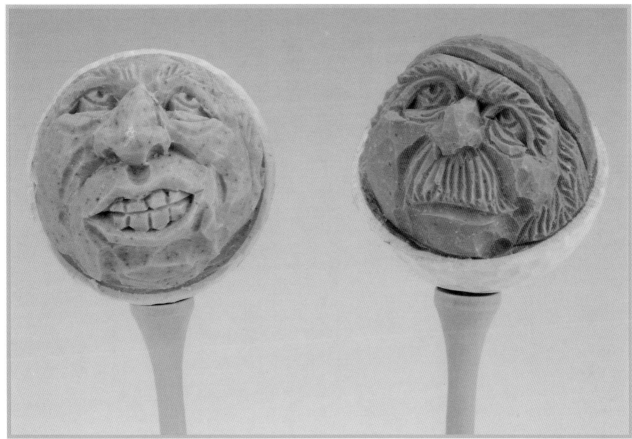

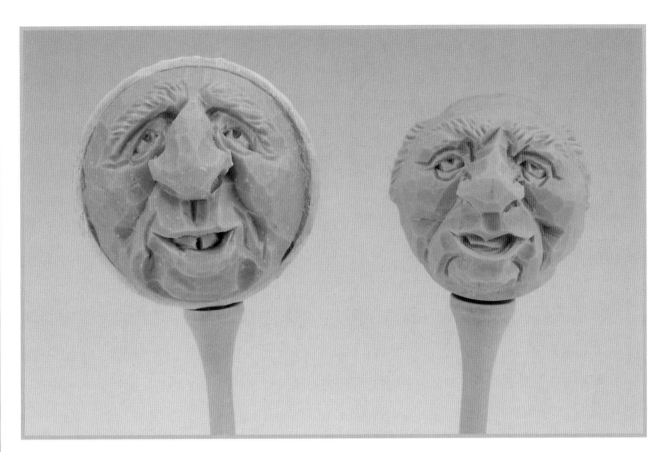

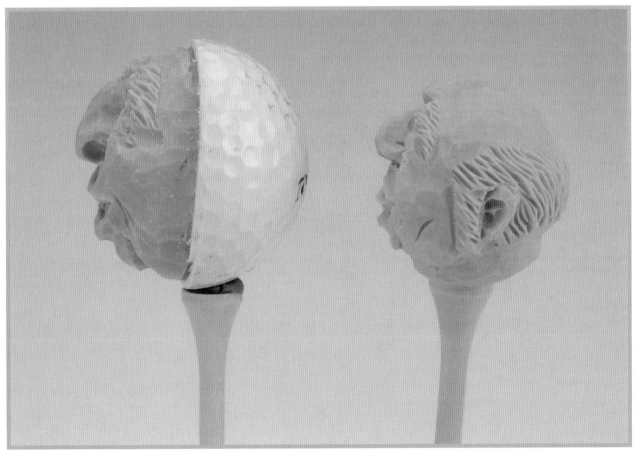

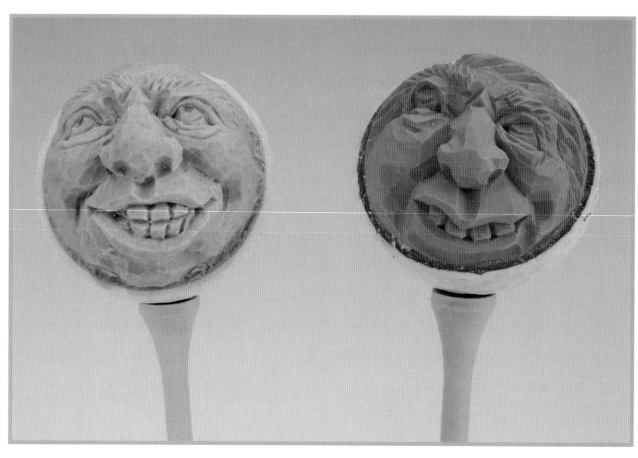

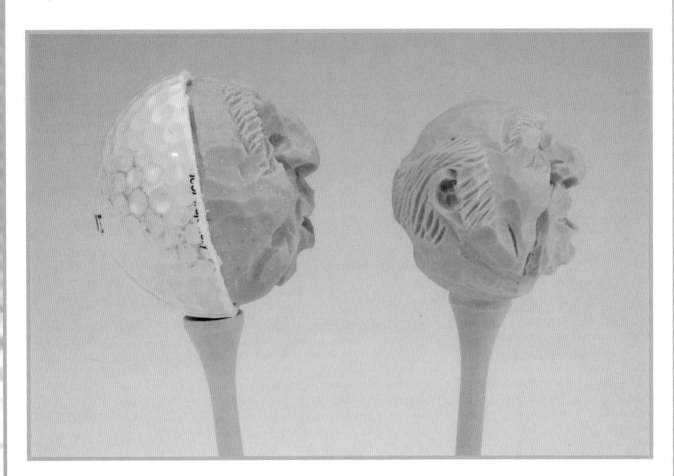